I'M GOOD AT
GEOGRAPHY
WHAT JOB CAN I GET?

Kelly Davis

Published in paperback in 2014 by Wayland
Copyright Wayland 2014

Wayland
Hachette Children's Books
338 Euston Road
London NW1 3BH

Wayland Australia
Level 17/207 Kent Street,
Sydney, NSW 2000

Commissioning editor: Victoria Brooker
Project editor: Kelly Davis
Designer: Tim Mayer
Picture research: Kelly Davis
Proofreader: Alice Harman

Produced for Wayland by
White-Thomson Publishing Ltd
www.wtpub.co.uk
+44 (0)843 2087 460

British Library Cataloguing in Publication Data
Davis, Kelly, 1959-
    I'm good at geography - what job can I get?.
    1. Geography–Vocational guidance–Juvenile
literature.
    I. Title
    910.2'3-dc23

ISBN-13: 9780750281836

Printed in China

10 9 8 7 6 5 4 3 2 1

Wayland is a division of Hachette Children's Books, an Hachette UK company
www.hachette.co.uk

Picture credits

1, Shutterstock/Diego Cervo; 3, Shutterstock/
Henryk Sadura; 4, Shutterstock/beboy; 5,
Shutterstock/neelsky; 6, Shutterstock/Arena
Creative; 7, Shutterstock/Dennis Sabo; 8,
Shutterstock/Stewart Smith Photography; 9,
Shutterstock/riekephotos; 10, Shutterstock/
Lentolo; 11, Shutterstock/Goodluz; 12,
Shutterstock/Yarchyk; 13, Dreamstime/
Tebnad; 14, Shutterstock/ronfromyork; 15,
Shutterstock/Lisa Young; 16, Shutterstock/
Clive Chilvers; 17, Dreamstime/Snyderdf; 18,
Dreamstime/Icefields; 19, Shutterstock/Dmitriy
Shironosov; 20, Shutterstock/Diego Cervo; 21,
Shutterstock/bluehand; 22 Shutterstock/Henryk
Sadura; 23, Shutterstock/AridOcean; 24,
Shutterstock/Scott Prokop; 25, Shutterstock/
Scott Prokop; 26, Shutterstock/saia; 27,
Dreamstime/Meryll; 28, Shutterstock/auremar;
29, Shutterstock/PhotoSky 4t com; cover
(top left), Shutterstock/Goodluz; cover (top
right), Shutterstock/Lentolo; cover (bottom),
Dreamstime/Snyderdf.

Disclaimer

CONTENTS

The world of geography

Geography covers many different aspects of life on Earth. Physical geography explores the natural environment, weather patterns, map-making, and how landscape features are formed. Human geography looks at the way people live in different parts of the world, how the global economy works, and how we can try to achieve a sustainable future for our planet. Because geography is such a wide-ranging subject, geography-related qualifications can lead to all sorts of careers.

Although geography is one of the humanities (like English and history), geographers use scientific and mathematical methods – for instance, when gathering the measurements and making the calculations needed to create maps and diagrams. For this reason, geography graduates are very versatile and highly valued by employers in many different areas, including transport, tourism, environmental protection, international aid, business and local government.

↑ Physical geography helps us understand dramatic events that occur in our environment, including earthquakes and volcanic eruptions.

Geography in the workplace

Many jobs – not just the obvious ones – require geographical knowledge and skills. For example, town planners need to be aware of infrastructure networks, and international aid workers have to be familiar with other cultures. Other careers, such as geology (the study of soil and rocks) and meteorology (the study of weather), require specialist knowledge of certain aspects of physical geography.

Special skills

To study geography or a geography-related subject at university, you will need very good A-level grades in geography and, preferably, maths or at least one science subject.

If you are good at geography, you will be interested in the world and concerned about environmental, scientific, social and political issues. You will be able to apply scientific principles and test theories, and have a thorough knowledge of information technology (IT). You will also be good at collecting and analysing data, writing reports and preparing maps and diagrams. These skills are useful for a wide range of jobs.

↓ Human geography gives us an insight into the very different lives of people in other parts of the world. These camel traders are at an annual fair in Rajasthan, India.

Tourism officer

If you are keen on geography, you may wish to travel and explore other places, both in the UK and abroad. Why not share your enthusiasm with others by becoming a tourism officer? Tourism is Britain's fifth-largest industry and it provides an increasing number of jobs. Whether dealing with foreign visitors or British tourists, tourism officers are central to the success of this industry.

They may work in a tourist information centre in a small town, helping visitors who want to know about local attractions or find a place to stay. Alternatively, they may be employed by a local authority to promote an entire region in an imaginative, creative way. For example, many more tourists have visited the windswept moors of West Yorkshire since the area became known as 'Brontë Country' – after the Victorian writers Charlotte, Emily and Anne Brontë.

↑ A tourism officer briefed the designer who created this striking graphic, featuring some of New York's most famous landmarks.

Job description

Tourism officers:

- inform the public about an attraction, town or region
- create marketing campaigns
- produce leaflets and update websites
- arrange surveys of visitors and analyse the results
- give presentations to community groups
- work with business owners and residents to support the local economy
- set up exhibitions to promote the local area
- organise and promote events and festivals.

What skills do I need?

It's sometimes possible to get a job as a tourism assistant without a degree but you will find it easier to become a tourism officer if you are a graduate in geography, tourism, tourism management or heritage. A relevant postgraduate qualification will also be very helpful. You will need to be good at talking to members of the public and writing promotional text. You should also be able to cope with pressure and having to do several things at once. Interest, enthusiasm and local knowledge are all important factors in securing a post.

PROFESSIONAL VIEWPOINT
'I've been working on a marketing campaign promoting our region for the last few months. We have several different music festivals each year and I've used them as the main focus for a supplement in a national newspaper. It's been very exciting!'
Samira, tourism officer

↓ Tourism officers can be involved in many different types of publicity. Here, a cable TV crew set up their cameras to make a tourism promotion film in the West Indies.

Park ranger

Most geographers enjoy being outdoors so working in a national park will be a very appealing option. There are 15 national parks in the UK, ranging from the Cairngorm mountains in Scotland to Dartmoor in Devon. These are particularly beautiful areas run by national park authorities, where nature and wildlife are protected by law. Some of the land is owned by the park authorities but much of it is owned by farmers and the National Trust. A great deal of the work in national parks is done by volunteers but there are also job opportunities for some professionals, including park rangers.

Job description

Park rangers:
- educate and inform the public about local wildlife and plants
- enforce regulations and by-laws
- do practical conservation work
- show visitors round the park
- negotiate rights of way
- resolve conflicts between visitors and other land users (such as farmers)
- help the emergency services – for example, if a member of the public needs to be rescued.

→ Park rangers have to be aware of possible dangers for visitors. For example, a shallow stream can turn into a raging torrent after heavy rain.

'Volunteering is really important. National park authorities want people who are motivated and hard-working. Doing voluntary work for a long period shows that you have what it takes. It took me four tries to get my job in the Brecon Beacons National Park but I'm glad I didn't give up.'
Peter, park ranger

Many people want to work in these stunning surroundings so there are usually a lot of applicants competing to get jobs in national parks. Park rangers (also known as park wardens) provide a link between the national park authority, visitors and local people. They conserve these areas – for instance, by monitoring erosion and arranging for litter to be removed. They also make it easier for visitors to come to the national parks by maintaining paths and providing information.

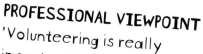
↓ Park rangers often use binoculars when monitoring local wildlife populations.

What skills do I need?

A degree in environmental management, conservation or geography is desirable, and you should always volunteer in a national park before applying for a paid position. A diploma in countryside management will certainly be an advantage. From a personal point of view, you need to enjoy being outdoors and be good at talking to a wide range of people and multi-tasking (doing several things at once).

Environmental consultant

Geography involves studying the environmental threats faced by our planet so you may well be interested in a career in this field. Environmental consultants advise individuals, companies and organisations on how to reduce the environmental impact of their activities and make them more sustainable, by decreasing the pollution they cause.

Environmental consultants need to consider different factors – wind farms are sustainable but many claim that they destroy a landscape's natural beauty.

Job description

Environmental consultants:

• do research and fieldwork to find out whether land, air or water is being polluted
• collect and interpret data gathered from a site
• assess the impact of pollution, for example on people living nearby
• suggest ways of reducing pollution
• have an up-to-date knowledge of laws relating to the environment
• write reports and make presentations.

PROFESSIONAL VIEWPOINT
'I've always been keen on the outdoors so I love the fact that I spend half my time on site, usually in my wellies! Between site visits, I'm at my computer, doing research, logging and interpreting the data we've collected, and writing reports.'
Melissa, environmental consultant

There are numerous interesting, varied job opportunities for environmental consultants, whether they are working for government departments or private construction or manufacturing companies. These range from helping to draft government policies on waste management to assessing the environmental impact of a new housing development or measuring the extent of pollution in a local river. Environmental consultants often have to find out about related subjects such as soil structure, groundwater drainage and the effects of certain harmful substances on human health.

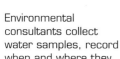

Environmental consultants collect water samples, record when and where they were taken, and send them to laboratories for analysis.

What skills do I need?

If you want to be an environmental consultant, you should ideally take A-levels in geography or environmental science, biology and chemistry, followed by a degree in an environment-related subject such as geography, geology, ecology, chemistry or environmental management. You can strengthen your application if you do a relevant postgraduate course and a work placement for a government agency. You should have good research and IT skills to analyse data, and be able to present your findings clearly and make effective presentations in meetings. If you progress to a senior level, you will also need to manage projects within a set time and budget.

Geologist

Many people who like physical geography are particularly interested in the science of geology, which explores the history and structure of our planet. You've probably seen geologists on television, striding up mountains and talking about volcanoes and earthquakes. You may also have seen palaeontologists (who study fossils), presenting programmes on dinosaurs. But most geologists are employed in other fields such as oil exploration, mining and quarrying, and the construction industry.

When geologists collect rock samples, they often split them open with a hammer in order to study their composition and look for fossils.

Job description

Geologists:
- carry out fieldwork and site visits
- collect rock and soil samples to be analysed
- consult geological maps
- research rock formations
- collect geological data
- produce geological reports
- attend academic and professional conferences
- manage budgets and staff for large projects.

Different types of geologist

Geoscientists interpret geological data to locate new oil and gas reserves, while wellsite geologists study soil samples from oil and gas wells and advise on how best to drill through particular types of rock. On building sites, environmental geologists check whether the land is polluted by dangerous chemicals, and engineering geologists assess whether the rocks are stable enough to build on. Hydrogeologists study the way water flows underground, while geochemists analyse soil and rock samples to check the age and composition of certain features. Geophysicists and seismologists collect data on seismic waves that may predict earthquakes.

What skills do I need?

You'll need a geography or geology A-level, combined with sciences or maths, in order to study geology at university. To become a professional geologist, a degree is essential – preferably in geology, geophysics or geotechnology, engineering geology, or mineral or mining engineering. A relevant postgraduate qualification will make you a stronger candidate for most geologists' posts. Geologists have to be very organised, practical and professional, and enjoy working as part of a team. You should be physically fit, have a driving licence, be prepared to work outdoors some of the time, and be good at summarising information and interpreting data.

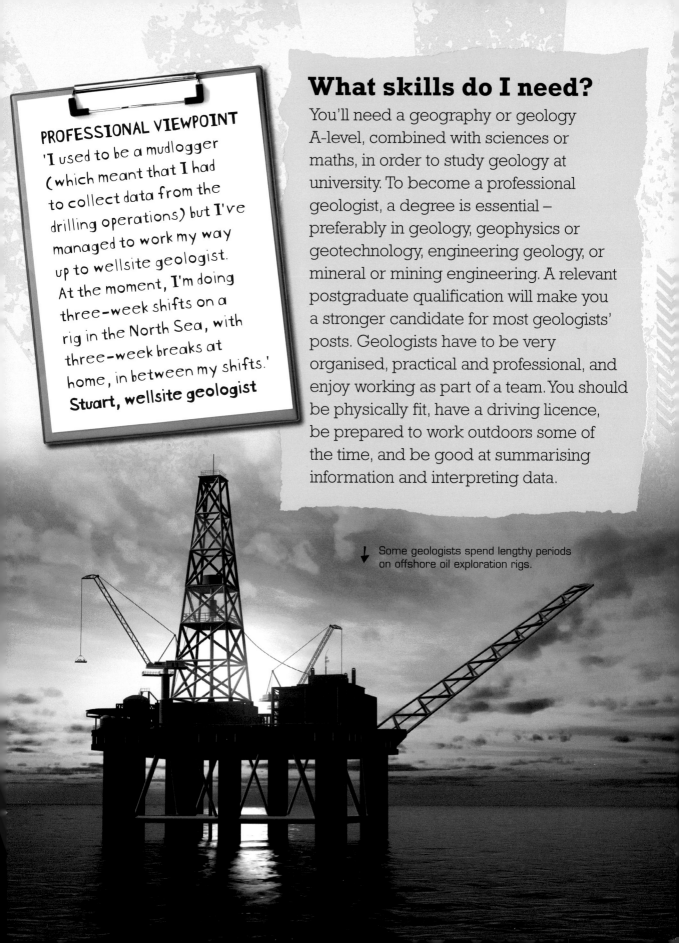

Some geologists spend lengthy periods on offshore oil exploration rigs.

Meteorologist

Physical geography includes the study of weather, and weather patterns affect our lives in many ways. Extreme weather conditions, such as floods, hurricanes and blizzards, cause huge problems around the world. The weather can also determine whether there is a good or a bad harvest. This affects farmers' income and, in turn, affects food prices for everyone. For all these reasons, meteorologists (scientists who specialise in weather forecasting) have an important job.

↑ Flood forecasts give people a chance to protect their property by placing sandbags in front of their doors.

Job description

Meteorologists:
- collect data such as satellite images (taken from space) and information from weather stations around the world
- take measurements, including temperature, air pressure and rainfall
- analyse weather data in order to compile weather reports
- use computer simulations to make short-range and long-range weather forecasts
- present TV, radio and online weather reports
- research changing weather patterns and their effects on the environment.

The Met Office is the UK's government-run national weather service and it employs more than 1,700 people at 60 locations around the world. The Met Office gathers information on the weather and the effects of climate change, and reports it to the public as well as to other companies and government agencies. Meteorologists also work for research centres, the armed forces, oil and gas suppliers, insurance companies, environmental consultancy firms, and the media.

What skills do I need?

Most employers of meteorologists want candidates with degrees in physics or maths. Meteorology, physical geography, environmental science, oceanography or computer science are also good choices if they are combined with physics or maths and a relevant postgraduate qualification. You will need to have a genuine interest in weather, and strong mathematical and computing skills. You should also be good at writing reports and working with other meteorologists and researchers.

A meteorologist tracking a hurricane on his computer points out its 'eye' (centre). This type of information is extremely helpful for the emergency services who have to evacuate the area.

PROFESSIONAL VIEWPOINT

'I've been fascinated by the weather since I was five years old, when a huge elm tree in our garden came down in a storm. That made a big impression on me! I took a joint honours degree in physical geography and physics and then worked at the Met Office for five years. They gave me the best possible training in weather forecasting.'

Barbara, TV weather presenter

International aid worker

Have you always had an urge to help other people? If you are keener on human geography than physical geography, you may well be interested in working for one of the many charities or non-governmental organisations (NGOs) that offer international aid. This type of work can involve many different activities, from organising short-term relief in response to a natural disaster to setting up long-term health and education projects in developing countries.

↓ Long-term education projects help to raise living standards across the world. Here, volunteers load up donated books that will be sent to Ghana.

Aid workers interview survivors of the 2010 hurricane in Haiti to find out how many have lost their homes and require emergency shelter.

People with all sorts of skills and backgrounds are needed in this field, both in the UK and abroad. For example, international aid jobs may be focused on the environment, infrastructure, healthcare, education or business development. Disaster relief usually involves urgent, short-term projects, such as providing food and shelter, and restoring clean water supplies and sanitation facilities after earthquakes and floods.

What skills do I need?

A degree in social sciences, international development, engineering, economics or a health-related subject will be helpful. However, it's sometimes possible to get a job in this field without a degree if you have a lot of relevant experience. Volunteering is vital, and there are many aid and development organisations that offer such opportunities. It will be an advantage to have one or more foreign languages in order to build relationships with people from other cultures. You should also be decisive, determined, outgoing, able to learn new skills quickly, and willing to travel and live in harsh conditions when necessary.

Transport planner

Transport networks (whether they are road, rail, air or sea) provide vital links between individuals and communities. Geographers study these interactions and consider the environmental impact of different types of transport. The British government wants to reduce car usage (in order to cut down on carbon emissions), and transport planners can play a key role by encouraging people to walk, cycle and make more use of public transport. If these issues concern you, why not become a transport planner?

↑ More people are likely to use bikes (rather than cars) if there are plenty of well-indicated cycle lanes.

Job description

Transport planners:

- research proposed transport projects
- analyse traffic statistics and measure costs and benefits of proposals
- use computer simulations to forecast the effects of planned improvements
- carry out public consultations on proposals
- work with designers on changes to transport infrastructure
- negotiate with transport companies, developers, local authorities and members of the public
- write funding applications
- write transport reports
- appear as witnesses in court during appeals against planning decisions.

What skills do I need?

It's best to have a degree, ideally in geography, environmental sciences, town planning, economics, business studies, mathematics, sociology or civil engineering. Some universities offer transport planning as a full or combined degree. Transport planners need to be good at solving problems and communicating with a wide range of people. You should also have excellent report writing, public speaking, numeracy and computer skills, as well as a keen interest in transport issues.

PROFESSIONAL VIEWPOINT

'I work for Transport for London and we put a lot of work into preparing for the London Olympics in 2012. We prioritised transport for athletes and Olympic Park workers, and there were a few hostile media reports at first because taxi drivers objected to some of the measures. But we gave the public plenty of advance warning about travel hotspots, and it all went well in the end.'

Jonathan, transport planner

Transport planners work for private companies (such as transport consultancies, and train and bus operators) as well as local authorities and government departments. Their work can range from planning a local cycle route to using computer simulations to predict the impact of a new motorway.

← Transport planners spend a lot of time discussing transport data, and how to improve existing networks and create new ones.

Travel writer

Most people who like geography have a burning desire to visit the places they've learned about. What better way to travel than to become a travel writer? You could be on safari in an African wildlife park one week, and cruising around the coast of Norway the next!

↓ Some research can be done on the Internet but most travel writers visit the places they are writing about.

Travel guides need to be updated regularly, to ensure that all the information they contain is accurate. This provides more work for travel writers.

Travel writers don't only write books about their own adventures; they also write guidebooks, leaflets and brochures, and articles for magazines and websites. Most travel writing is done on a freelance (self-employed) basis, but there are some full-time jobs available for journalists on newspapers and magazines.

What skills do I need?

You may have a degree in geography, travel and tourism, English, media studies or journalism, but it's not essential to be a graduate to succeed as a travel writer. Experience and ability are particularly important, and you may have to start by offering to do some unpaid work for a local newspaper or magazine. Writing your own travel blog is another good way to gain experience and demonstrate your writing ability to prospective employers. Travel writers need to be interested in people and places both in the UK and around the world. You should be able to write in a lively, original way that will encourage people to visit the places you describe. Knowledge of IT and an enthusiastic, determined personality will also be helpful.

PROFESSIONAL VIEWPOINT

'I've built up good relationships with the editors of a few well-known magazines and they often take my articles – but not always. You have to be quite thick-skinned and not take offence if they turn you down. Being a freelancer means working odd hours and having an irregular income but I feel lucky to be able to visit so many amazing places.'

Edward, travel writer

Cartographer

If you like geography, you've probably always loved looking at maps. Cartographers produce maps, diagrams and charts for many different purposes. Whether you are planning a country walk, studying an endangered animal or working out where to drill for oil or gas, maps provide vital information.

In the UK, the Ordnance Survey is a major employer of cartographers. There are also jobs available in government departments, the armed services, public utilities (such as water, gas and electricity companies) and private publishing companies.

Job description

Cartographers:
- design layouts needed for maps, diagrams and charts
- choose typefaces, symbols and colours
- research, collect and analyse data
- use computer software to produce maps based on satellite images and aerial photographs
- work with geographical information systems (GIS)
- check the accuracy of maps and charts
- keep up to date with the latest mapping software
- manage large-scale mapping projects.

➡ Land surveyors visit the area to be mapped and measure the exact position of features on the ground.

Maps have traditionally been based on information gathered by land surveyors. Nowadays, this data is more frequently collected from the air, using satellite images and aerial photography. Geographical information systems or GIS (see pages 24–25) are used to model and analyse landscape features and to present statistics. Hundreds of years ago, maps were drawn by hand and all cartographers had to be skilled artists. Now they are almost always produced using information technology (IT). New maps are often created by combining and altering existing maps.

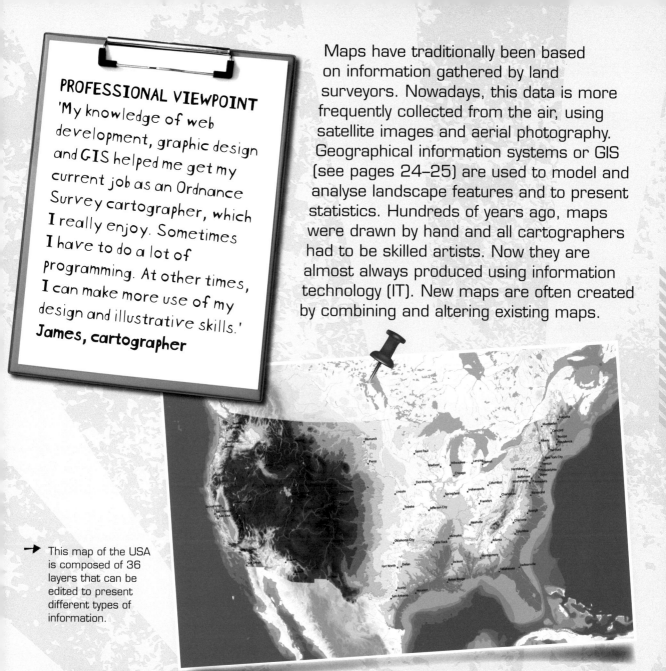

➡ This map of the USA is composed of 36 layers that can be edited to present different types of information.

What skills do I need?

Most cartography jobs require a degree, preferably in geographical information systems (GIS), computer science, physics, chemistry, maths, geology or earth sciences, geography, geophysics, marine sciences, surveying, urban studies, engineering or graphic design. Cartographers need good IT and design skills as well as the ability to work independently and solve problems. It's also helpful if you are the kind of person who pays close attention to detail.

Geographical information systems officer

Geographical information systems (GIS) are used to store, analyse and present complex geographical data. This computerised data can help professionals plan and deliver products and services in many areas, including transport, healthcare, construction, defence, water and electricity. GIS is therefore a very fast-growing field, offering many career opportunities both in the UK and abroad. A GIS officer is an IT professional who uses a computerised system to process geographical data.

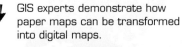

PROFESSIONAL VIEWPOINT

'There's always more to learn about GIS, as there are new developments in the field all the time, and that makes my job very challenging. I've been working for a consultancy firm for the last two years. Now that I have more experience, I'm being given some really interesting long-term projects for big corporate clients.'

Sarah, GIS officer

GIS experts demonstrate how paper maps can be transformed into digital maps.

The increasing use of the global positioning system (GPS) is leading to new GIS applications. GPS, a space-based satellite navigation system that can find almost any location on Earth, was first developed by the US Defense Department in the 1970s. This technology is now used in mobile phones, and it can be combined with GIS in many innovative ways. For example, GPS tools can be used to locate areas that are vulnerable to flooding, and GIS can then be used to present this information in map form for a government or local authority.

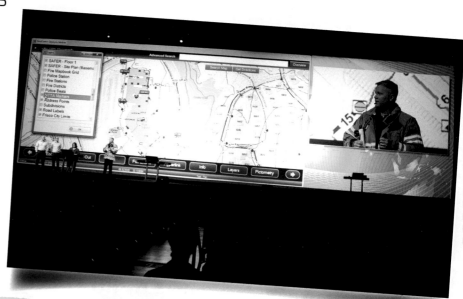

↑ The world's biggest GIS conference is held every year in San Diego, California. This presentation, at the 2010 conference, was on GIS applications for the US fire service.

What skills do I need?

Any graduate can enter this field but employers will favour those with degrees in GIS, geography or computer science. GIS officers need to have a good knowledge of maths and IT, strong interpersonal and communication skills, and cartographical and technical ability. You should also pay attention to detail and be decisive, motivated and capable of carrying out independent research.

Job description

GIS officers:
- convert paper maps into GIS data
- develop computer programs to transfer GIS data from one system to another
- present GIS data on company websites
- use GIS data to investigate patterns, such as trends in population growth or consumer spending
- work with clients on particular projects and find out exactly what information they require and in what form.

Town planner

Geography explores the built environment – villages, towns and cities – as well as the natural landscape, so you may like the idea of a career in town planning. Town planners have a major impact on community life, and sometimes have to make controversial decisions. For instance, there is a great shortage of affordable housing in the UK at present, partly because people are living longer and more people are living on their own. Town planners have to balance this demand for more houses against the need for 'green space' for leisure activities and nature conservation.

Town planners make use of three-dimensional computerised layouts like this one when they are working out their designs.

Some planners work in less densely populated, rural areas, where the issues are different from those in built-up urban areas. But wherever they work, they are faced with the demands of business and local communities, which sometimes conflict with each other. Town planners also have to consider the effects of climate change and try to ensure that any development is appropriate and sustainable.

➡ New developments can involve repairing or replacing underground sanitation pipes. Town planners need to take this into account when working out a schedule.

Job description

Town planners:

- assess planning applications
- have a knowledge of planning laws
- consult with architects, surveyors, developers and the public to resolve planning problems
- design layouts using GIS, computer aided design (CAD) and other IT systems
- make presentations on developments
- write reports on effects of developments.

What skills do I need?

The preferred qualification is a degree in planning, accredited by the Royal Town Planning Institute (see page 31). Alternatively, you could do a degree in a subject such as geography, urban studies or architecture, followed by a postgraduate course in planning. You will need strong communication, negotiating, problem-solving and organisational skills, and you should be able to work well with other planners, administrative staff and local government officials. Flexibility, creativity and attention to detail will also be very useful qualities in this role. Try to get some work experience with your local authority (preferably in the planning department) before you apply to university.

Geography teacher

Would you like to pass on your love of geography to others? Perhaps you want to help children develop an understanding of other cultures or the environmental issues our society is facing? Or maybe you like the idea of teaching them about weather patterns, or the way the Earth was formed billions of years ago?

PROFESSIONAL VIEWPOINT
'I really love taking my sixth formers on field trips. Last year, I took an A2 group to Iceland and they saw all the features they had been learning about – huge glaciers, boiling mud pools, active volcanoes, lava flows. I'm sure they will remember it for the rest of their lives!'
Liz, geography teacher

↑ Teaching geography can be very rewarding, as the subject is so clearly relevant to pupils' own lives.

Job description

Geography teachers:
- plan interesting, stimulating lessons
- use a variety of teaching resources, such as interactive whiteboards
- manage pupils' behaviour
- monitor pupils' progress and mark their work
- co-operate with teaching colleagues
- communicate with pupils' parents
- research new topics
- keep up to date with curriculum developments
- organise field trips and outings.

What skills do I need?

There are several ways of becoming a geography teacher. You can take a geography degree and then do initial teacher training (ITT) or a Postgraduate Certificate of Education (PGCE) for a year. Alternatively, you can study for your degree and complete your ITT at the same time. Taking the Bachelor of Arts (BA) with qualified teacher status (QTS) will enable you to specialise in geography. If you would rather teach in primary schools, you could do the general Bachelor of Education (BEd) honours degree. Most importantly, you should have a real enthusiasm for geography. Like all teachers, you also need to have strong leadership skills and be well organised and good at communicating. Being patient and self-confident will help you cope with challenging pupils. You can gain experience of working with children by doing private tutoring or helping at a play scheme, youth club or summer camp.

Primary schools usually concentrate on the core skills of numeracy and literacy, with only occasional coverage of geography topics. As a specialist geography teacher, you are therefore more likely to work in a secondary school, teaching children aged 11 to 18. You could also work in a sixth form college or further education college.

 Field trips involve a lot of planning to ensure that children are safe while they are learning and having fun.

Glossary

aerial photography photographs taken from an aircraft or spacecraft

analyse study or examine in detail

appropriate (of development) suitable; matching its surroundings

by-law local law or regulation

carbon emission output of carbon dioxide, a gas that traps heat coming from the Earth's surface and thereby contributes to a gradual warming of the planet's atmosphere

computer simulation computer program that imitates (models) a process in the real world

controversial likely to cause arguments

culture attitudes, customs and behaviour of a particular group of people

data factual information

erosion process by which soil and rocks are worn away, for example by a great many people walking on a surface for a long time

fossil trace of an ancient insect, animal or plant that has been preserved in the Earth's crust

fossil fuel energy source (such as coal or oil) formed millions of years ago from the remains of fossilised animals and plants

freelance self-employed

infrastructure basic services needed by a community, such as water and power supplies and transportation systems

marketing type of business concerned with publicity, promotion and advertising

National Trust organisation set up to preserve historic buildings and areas of great beauty in England, Wales and Northern Ireland

non-governmental organisation (NGO) non-profit-making organisation with social or political aims, such as a charity, community group or campaigning organisation

oil and gas reserves supplies of oil or gas that are known to exist deep underground or under the sea

Ordnance Survey British government agency that deals with cartography (map-making)

pollution contamination of water, air or soil through disposal of harmful waste

post job

postgraduate after a first degree

right of way legal right to take a route through property belonging to someone else

rural relating to the countryside

sanitation provision of clean water and removal of waste or sewage

satellite spacecraft used to collect information or for communication

seismic wave vibration, generated by an earthquake, that travels through the Earth's crust and can be measured

statistic piece of factual information expressed in number form

sustainable possible to maintain and continue

theory idea about how something works

urban relating to towns or cities

versatile able to do many different things

Further information

There are many specific courses, apprenticeships and jobs using geographical skills, so where do you go to find out more? It is really useful to meet up with careers advisers at school or college and to attend careers fairs to see the range of opportunities. Remember that public libraries and newspapers are other important sources of information. The earlier you check out your options, the better prepared you will be to put your geographical skills to good use as you earn a living in future.

Books

Careers Using Geography, Patrick Talbot, Kogan Page, 2000

So You Want to Work in the Travel and Tourism Industry, Margaret McAlpine, Wayland, 2008

Travel and Tourism Careers (In the Workplace), Kaye Stearman, Amicus, 2010

What Next After School?: All You Need to Know About Work, Travel and Study, Elizabeth Holmes, Kogan Page, 2012

Websites

www.prospects.ac.uk/options_geography_job_options.htm
A very useful guide to geography-related careers, with a comprehensive list of contacts and resources.

www.rgs.org/OurWork/Study+Geography/Careers
The Royal Geographical Society website offers helpful careers advice, including career profiles.

www.bgs.ac.uk/vacancies/careers.htm
The British Geological Survey website careers section has video interviews and case studies.

www.cartography.org.uk
The British Cartographic Society website. Click on 'About cartography' to access careers advice.

www.education.gov.uk/get-into-teaching
The Department for Education Teaching Agency website offers guidance on different routes into teaching.

www.metoffice.gov.uk/about-us/
The Met Office website explains the work of the Met Office. Go to the 'Learning' section to find information on the training offered by the Met Office College.

www.rtpi.org.uk
This is the Royal Town Planning Institute website, which has a list of accredited qualifications in town planning. Click on 'Education and careers'.

www.nationalparks.gov.uk
A fascinating website that tells you everything you need to know about working and volunteering in national parks.

Index